ICE HOCKEY LOGOS

COLORING BOOK

OTTAWA SENATORS

NEW YORK ISLANDERS

NEW JERSEY DEVILS

LOS ANGELES KINGS

FLORIDA PANTHERS

EDMONTON OILERS

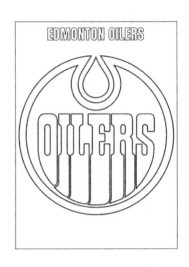

CHICAGO BLACKHAWKS

COLORADO AVALANCHE

COLUMBUS BLUE JACKETS

THIS BOOK BELONGS TO:

WINNIPEG JETS

WASHINGTON CAPITALS

VANCOUVER CANUCKS

TORONTO MAPLE LEAFS

TORONTO
MAPLE
LEAFS

TAMPA BAY LIGHTNING

ST LOUIS BLUES

SAN JOSE SHARKS

PITTSBURGH PENGUINS

PHILADELPHIA FLYERS

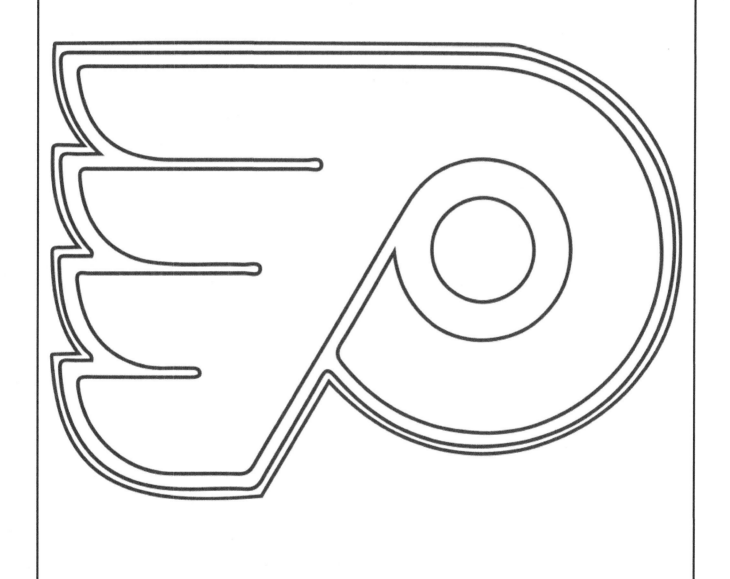

NEW YORK RANGERS

NEW YORK ISLANDERS

NEW JERSEY DEVILS

NASHVILLE PREDATORS

MONTREAL CANADIENS

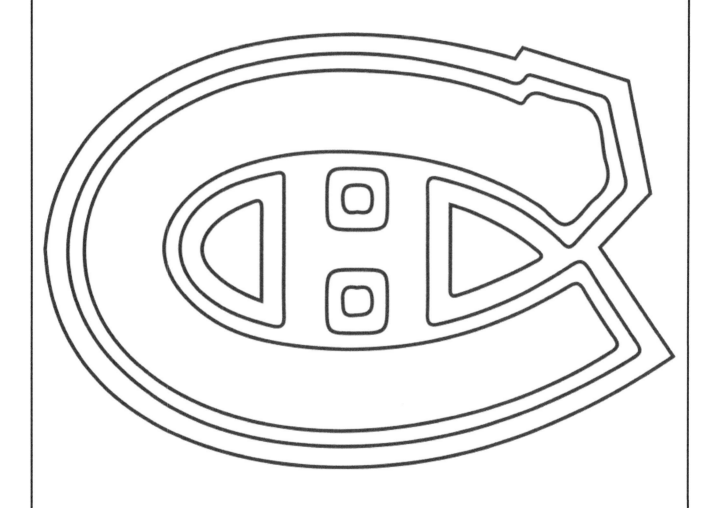

MINNESOTA WILD

LOS ANGELES KINGS

FLORIDA PANTHERS

EDMONTON OILERS

DETROIT RED WINGS

DALLAS STARS

COLUMBUS BLUE JACKETS

COLORADO AVALANCHE

CHICAGO BLACKHAWKS

CAROLINA HURRICANES

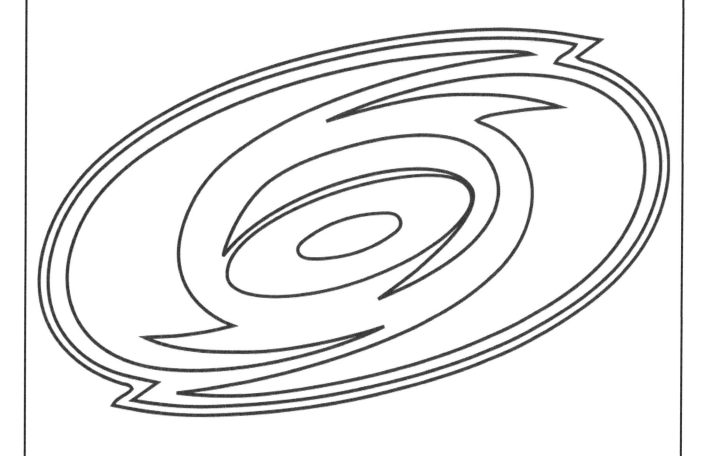

CALGARY FLAMES

BUFFALO SABRES

BOSTON BRUINS

ARIZONA COYOTES

ANAHEIM DUCKS

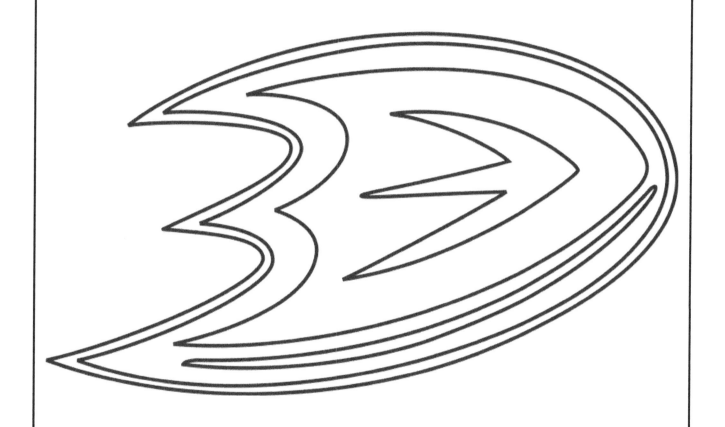

Made in the USA
Monee, IL
03 November 2024

69205864R00039